Try a superhero pos

THE CONFIDENCE WORKBOOK

A Kid's Activity Book for Dealing with Low Self-Esteem

Go on a rainbow walk

Fill in a smile-a-day journal

Make a lucky charm

IMOGEN HARRISON

Foreword by Amanda Ashman-Wymbs,
BA (Hons) BACP accredited Counselor and Psychotherapist

SKY PONY PRESS

Sky Pony Press
New York

First published as *The Confidence Workbook* in the United Kingdom by Summersdale Publishers, an imprint of Octopus Publishing Book.

First Skyhorse edition, 2022.

Visit our website at www.skyponypress.com.

10 9 8 7 6 5 4 3 2 1

Manufactured in China, July 2022
This product conforms to CPSIA 2008

Library of Congress Cataloging-in-Publication Data is available on file.

Text by Poppy O'Neill
Interior and cover design by Summersdale Publishers Ltd.
US edition editor: Nicole Frail

Print ISBN: 978-1-5107-7274-8

Printed in China

This book belongs to...

_____

Contents

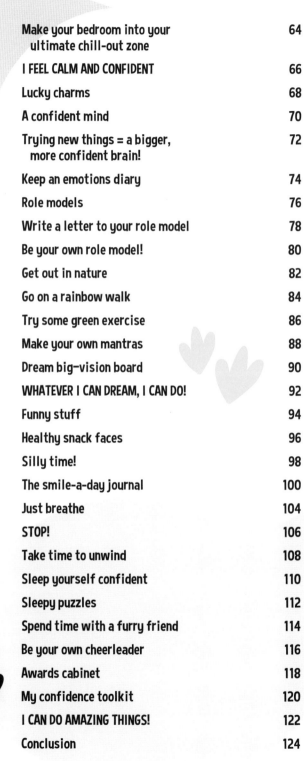

FOREWORD

By Amanda Ashman-Wymbs,
BA (Hons) BACP accredited Counselor and Psychotherapist

When I reflect on my work with children over the years, and my experience as a mother of two girls, I can see how important having healthy self-esteem and self-confidence is to a child's resilience and psychological and emotional well-being.

It is essential to support children to increase and develop their self-confidence so they can achieve their potential and learn how to express themselves. *The Confidence Workbook* is a brilliant resource for parents and other caring adults in supporting children who may need extra help with confidence. It is full of fun activities and techniques that children can do on their own or with an adult, which will help them access and build a positive self-image and learn how to express themselves.

The content supports children to focus on their strengths, to become more aware of their thought patterns and emotions, and even offers some simple neuroscience. There are sections on developing empathy and gratitude, and practicing mindfulness and environmental connection, all of which will support a child's personal growth.

I can highly recommend this workbook, which is packed with lots of creative activities and also draws on more structured therapeutic methods that are presented in a way that is friendly, digestible, and fun for children.

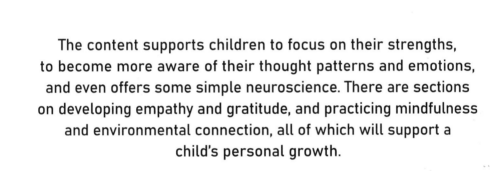

Welcome,
parents and caregivers!

We all want our children to feel confident and feel good about themselves so that they can really make the most of the opportunities that come their way. We also want them to have the courage to speak up for themselves and forge lasting friendships. But, as we know, confidence isn't something you are born with; it's something that must be nurtured and grows with use, like a muscle. This book will provide the tools for your child to grow their confidence and keep it at a healthy level. We'll look at how to speak and act with confidence as well as ways to boost inner confidence with positive self-talk, using mindfulness and cognitive behavioral therapy techniques.

We'll also look at what affects confidence—this is unique to everyone. By working through some fun, creative tasks, your child will be able to create their very own confidence toolkit that will set them up to be mentally strong and resilient for life.

You know your child best, and you may wish to work with them on the activities, but let them speak, and be careful not to influence their responses. The best way to support them is through active listening so that your child feels safe expressing themselves to you. Let them have their say and respond by using body language to show you are listening and understanding. When the moment's right, paraphrase what they have said, showing they have your full attention. You don't need to agree with your child—a lot of worries can be irrational—but you can still affirm and empathize with them.

If your child would prefer not to write down or discuss specific thoughts, the themes in the book can be explored through drawing and painting, role play, building blocks, singing songs, dancing to music, or making mud pies—whatever captures your child's imagination. Research has found expressing difficult emotions through creative play is one of the most effective ways for children to process their feelings and improve their mental health.

Look out for the parent/caregiver and child icons, as these act as signposts for more technical information about the relevance and usefulness of a specific activity.

HI THERE!

Welcome to your very own confidence activity book! This is the place where you will learn some amazing life skills to help you grow your self-confidence and have lots of fun along the way. Having confidence feels great and gives us the courage to be ourselves and do the things that we want to do. It's something we all have to work at, and the good news is that we all have the power within us to be more confident.

Sometimes it can seem really hard to feel confident. There are many reasons for this, and it's different for everyone. Confidence fluctuates, and we can be confident about some things while being less confident about others. The main thing, though, is to develop a healthy underlying confidence to carry you through every day.

Here are some questions to ask yourself:
Do you often . . .

- feel scared to try new things?

- find it hard to speak up?

- feel unconfident about making new friends?

- think that things will always go wrong for you?

If you're nodding your head while reading this list, you've come to the right place. This book is here to show you what you can do to feel more confident. Fun challenges and activities include designing your own coat of arms, writing a letter to your role model, going on a rainbow walk, breathing exercises you can do with a slice of pizza (yes, really!), and so much more.

By the end of the book, you will have created your own personal confidence toolkit—a list of simple but effective techniques that work for you whenever you need a boost of courage or a reminder that you are unique and special.

Take your grown-up along for the ride, because there are special tips throughout for them to read with you if you want, and activities that could be fun to do together! Look for this icon for these special tips:

Let's get cracking!

LET'S TALK ABOUT IT

When we're not sure about something or feel nervous or unhappy, talking to someone about it can really help. On this page, draw your favorite people that you feel comfortable talking to.

If you don't feel confident about talking, you can always write a note.

Name: ....

Name: ....

Name: ....

Name: ....

13

What I LOVE about being ME

There's no one quite like you and there never will be— isn't that an amazing thought?

Sometimes we forget how wonderful we are, so for this activity, let's shine a light on your greatness!

In order to grow your confidence, it's important to recognize the things that make you feel good about yourself—no matter how big or small. You could be the best at cuddles or drawing dogs, be a kind and caring friend, or have a talent for cartwheels or swimming. Focusing on the things you like about yourself helps you break the habit of thinking you're not good enough. Nurturing this positive self-image can make you feel capable and excited about trying new things.

Write down ten great things about you on the leaves of this tree, and when you have filled those leaves, draw some more so you can write even more things and feel your self-confidence soar! Keep on adding leaves to the tree any time you like and watch the tree grow!

14

15

THE POWER OF POSITIVITY

Words are powerful and magical—just look at all the confident words swirling around Captain Confident! Every morning, she does a ritual to give herself the confidence to face the day's challenges. Her secret is to say positive affirmations out loud.

Positive affirmations are phrases or statements that:

- ✔ Challenge the voice in your head that says you can't do something
- ✔ Motivate you to try something new
- ✔ Give you a confidence boost
- ✔ Help you change the things in your life that you don't like

. . . because Captain Confident knows it's important to appreciate yourself and recognize that you are wonderful, just as you are!

Write down some affirmations of your own to say out loud. You can start by circling your favorite ones around Captain Confident!

My happy thoughts make me happy inside and out

I can do anything I set my mind to

I am always brave enough to try

I am smart

Positive affirmations have been proven to encourage a more healthy mindset. When we think more positively, we're less likely to dwell on things that make us feel down about ourselves, enabling us to feel more hopeful and optimistic instead.

VISUALIZE A MORE CONFIDENT YOU

Feeling low in confidence has nothing to do with courage or personal strength—you have these things in large amounts! It's also important to know that everyone feels nervous or shy sometimes so you're never alone in feeling this way.

When starting out on your confidence journey, it helps to visualize what a more confident you will look like and the sorts of things that a more confident you will enjoy doing. Perhaps you want to try a new hobby or make a new friend or invite a friend for a sleepover. Confidence can change your view of the world, and it offers many opportunities to learn, make friends, and flourish.

Let's build this more confident you. On the facing page, write down a list of ten things that you want to try but don't currently feel you have the confidence to. This is your special list, and by the end of this book, you will have acquired the tools to GO FOR IT!

Confidence coat of arms

What makes you great? Have a look back at the things that you love about you from pages 14 and 15 for some ideas and see if you can fill this coat of arms with images that symbolize your individual skills, talents, and character traits.

Having a coat of arms has been a sign of prestige throughout history, and symbols were chosen to represent the finest qualities of a country, an organization, a family, or an individual. Here are some symbols and their meanings that you might like to use on your coat of arms.

Lion — bravery

Fish — a good friend

Dolphin — speedy

Fox — witty

Mermaid — good singer

Phoenix — winner

Unicorn — courage and strength

Dragon — caring

Bells — kind

Feathers — calm

Hands — honest

Shell — loves to travel

Bay leaves — artistic

Anchor — hopeful

Torch — wise

22

Add some elements that are unique to you, such as your initials and images of your favorite hobbies.

"OOPS!" MOMENTS

We all have times when we think "Oops! Why did I say/do that?" and those moments, depending on how we respond to them, can affect whether we want to try those things again.

Everyone makes mistakes—even grown-ups—and rather than feeling regret and wishing you could go back and do things differently, or wishing that you hadn't tried in the first place, there is a much better way of looking at mistakes.

The messy oops on these pages look like mistakes, but can you make something new out of them?

Hmm, is this a butterfly?

reminds me
of a slug

Mistakes help us learn and
grow, and they can lead us to find
much better solutions to our problems.
The next time you make a mistake, be
kind to yourself and see it as a
stepping stone to learning how
to do something better.

Remember: don't be too hard on yourself. You
don't have to be perfect. Just do your best and
give yourself credit for the things you do well
and the things you're working hard at.

 # Change negative thoughts into positive ones

One of the best things you can do to grow your self-confidence is to switch your negative thoughts into positive ones. Your thoughts are powerful. They can affect your mood and how your body feels. That's why it's important to remember you can change how you feel just by changing your thoughts! When we think kind and reassuring thoughts about ourselves, this is called positive self-talk. For example, imagine you have just dropped a glass of juice on the carpet. It's easy to say to yourself, "I'm so stupid for doing this!" and make yourself feel bad, when a kinder and more reassuring thing to say to yourself would be, "I made a mistake here, but I will be more careful the next time I carry a drink."

Try the Be Kind to Your Mind Challenge when you turn the page. You can do this!

Remember: always speak kindly to yourself because you are the one who is listening!

Saying and thinking nice things about yourself will give you a big confidence boost. If you do it every day, it can make you less worried or nervous as well as improve your overall health and well-being.

BE KIND TO YOUR MIND CHALLENGE

Over the next five days, write down every time you catch yourself thinking a negative thought about your abilities, achievements, or anything that might make you feel down about yourself or less confident.

Then see how you can rewrite these mean thoughts into positive ones. You might find it helps to work with your grown-up on this task. The most important thing to remember is to be kind to your mind in the same way you would be kind to a friend! It's so important to get in the habit of saying nice things to yourself, as it helps you pick yourself up again more readily when things don't go as hoped or bad stuff happens. This is called resilience, and having this special skill will help you your whole life.

	Negative voice	Positive voice
	I made loads of mistakes in English today.	I did my best in English today, but I will practice so that next time I will do better, because I'm good at it.
DAY 1		
DAY 2		
DAY 3		
DAY 4		
DAY 5		

The compliments collector

Compliments are nice things that we say to someone or that someone says to us. Compliments are precious and important because they can make us feel special, confident, and happy, and the great thing about them is we can always go back to them so we can feel those good feelings all over again.

Collect and store your compliments in the fluttery butterflies on the facing page, or copy them and cut them out so they can flutter freely on your bedroom wall.

Saving compliments by writing them down and keeping a visual record is a great way to give your self-confidence a boost, especially if you have them to hand or in mind when you need a little courage before trying something that you might feel nervous or unsure about. Also, it's important to remember the power of your words and how complimenting someone else can give them a self-confidence boost too! What sort of things could you say to your favorite people today? Write them down here.

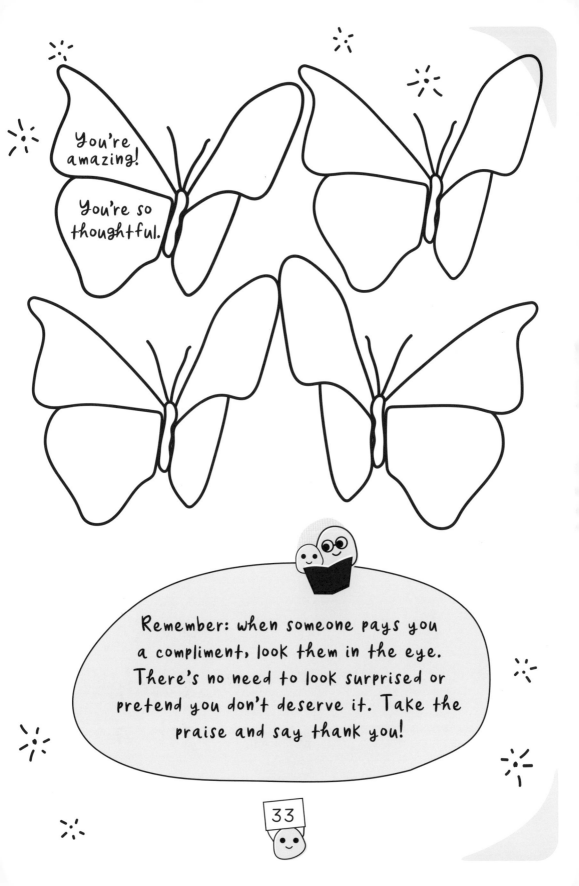

The Superhero Challenge

We all love to be treated kindly by others and to receive compliments and praise for our efforts and achievements, as it can give us a real confidence boost. The great thing is that when we carry out kind acts and give compliments to others, we actually benefit as much as the person receiving the kindness. Acts of kindness—whether you are the giver or receiver— release feel-good chemicals in the brain that make you feel happy.

How can you show kindness to others? Are you ready to take the Superhero Challenge? A cape and mask are optional but, if you want to design your own superhero outfit, it's up to you! Draw your outfit on the opposite page. What colors would you choose to make you dazzle? And, most importantly, what would your name be? Here are some words to help you work it out. Circle the words that best describe you!

LOVELY caring smart kind TIDY clever courageous SPARKLY SHINY strong super calm arty QUIET TOUGH NOISY HAPPY

DRAW YOUR SUPERHERO OUTFIT

WRITE YOUR SUPERHERO NAME HERE:

_____

Are you ready for the challenge? Over the next five days, see how many acts of kindness you can do for friends, family, and other people who you know in your community. Ask your parent or caregiver first before embarking on your Superhero Challenges.

Remember: these don't need to be big acts of kindness; small things mean so much too!

Fill in the Superhero Challenge chart and watch your confidence bloom!

Monday	Tuesday	Wednesday

Thursday	Friday	Saturday	Sunday

Putting yourself in someone else's shoes is an expression that's often used to describe seeing a situation from another person's point of view. This is a good practice when it comes to understanding others and can offer up ideas for something you could do to support them, or a small act of kindness that they might appreciate.

We all need a confidence boost sometimes, and this is where looking the part comes in. You might not have even considered this before, but how you hold yourself—how you stand or sit—affects how you feel. Why is this? Well, it's because your muscles are directly connected to the emotional centers of your brain, or, to put it another way:

When we look confident, we feel confident!

So, just making small changes to how you stand or move can give you a big boost and make you feel more confident.

Strike a pose—according to scientists, standing in a powerful or winning pose for 2 minutes can give you an instant confidence boost. Try some of these poses and see how much better you feel!

Winning pose–
stand with your feet apart and your hands in the air, like you've scored the winning goal in the match.

40

Power pose— stand with one hand on your hip and the other out in front, with your head held high.

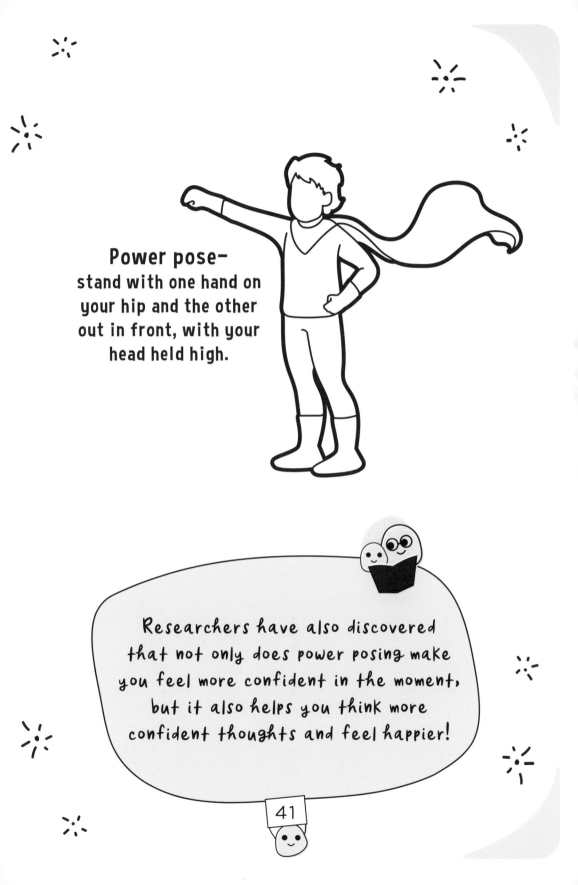

Researchers have also discovered that not only does power posing make you feel more confident in the moment, but it also helps you think more confident thoughts and feel happier!

JUST SMILE!

When we smile, it makes us and everyone around us feel better.
But a smile can do so much more than that:

- 🙂 Smiling can make us feel more confident and tells others that we are friendly.
- 🙂 Smiling is a mood booster—when you smile, it tells your brain that it's time to release endorphins (your happy hormones).
- 🙂 Smiling is contagious—when you smile at others, they more often than not will smile back!
- 🙂 Smiling makes others feel comfortable.
- 🙂 Smiling makes people want to talk to you and listen to what you have to say.

So, when you find that you need a quick
confidence boost, try smiling!

Add some smiles to these furry friends!

Look into my eyes!

When you meet someone, what's the first thing you tend to do? Hopefully it's look them in the eye and smile, and perhaps say a friendly, "Hello!" These simple greetings set the tone for new friendships to be made, and friends give you confidence and make life fun! Take a look in the mirror and draw your smiling face as if you're meeting yourself for the first time. See how it makes you look confident and ready to face whatever challenges lie ahead.

Scholars say that the eyes are the windows of the soul. Take a good look at your eyes and color in the eye below with all the colors that you see. You will be amazed how intricate and beautiful they are.

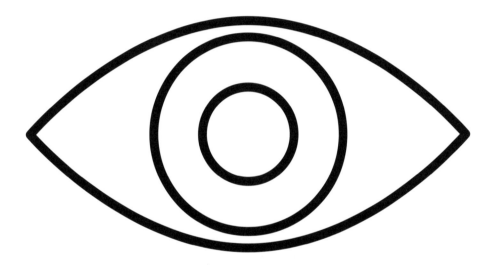

SET THE TONE

Our voices and the tone of them can say a lot about how confident we are feeling. When we are feeling nervous or shy, we might speak quietly or too quickly, or struggle to get the words out. Everyone experiences this sometimes, so you are not alone. There are some simple things you can do to help you become a more confident speaker.

- **Get talking** at home—around the dinner table, on the walk to school, in the car. Use these opportunities to offer opinions, ask questions, tell jokes—whatever you want to say, say it! The more you speak, the more confident you will become.

- **Get talking** while out and about—for example, see if you can make a purchase with someone at a till, where the conversation will be specific and manageable.

- **Get talking** at school—see how much you can learn about your friends by asking questions and then tell them all about yourself and your interests too.

- **Small performances**—see if you can practice a poem or a song and then perform it for your family.

RANDOM WORDS GENERATOR

Here's a fun game to play with your grown-up or a group of friends or family to get you talking. Copy the random words below, or create your own list on a piece of paper and cut them out. Then, find a small box or a tin to put them in. Now take turns picking out a word and talk about the random object for 1 minute—it can be a description of the item or a memory or made-up story. This game will help you become quick-thinking and will give you the confidence to speak more easily and fluently during a conversation.

icicle	seaweed	angel
chocolate coin	cave	snail
cat	hotel	TV remote
snow-capped mountain	summer	dog bowl
oak tree	holiday	orangutan
playground	top hat	towel
teacher	joke	plant pot
seashore	seagull	ship

When we don't feel confident about speaking, we might choose not to speak at all in situations that make us nervous. Some people who have to give speeches as part of their job practice by using tongue twisters to help them speak more clearly and confidently. Tongue twisters are fun and effective exercises for your mouth to prepare it and you for speaking up and speaking out. Try these out to help you feel more confident about speaking up. It's also a really funny thing to do with your grown-up. See who can say them correctly and in the quickest time. Good luck!

She sees cheese.

I saw a kitten eating chicken in the kitchen.

FRED
fed
TED
bread.

Six
slimy
snails
slid slowly seaward.

I scream,
you scream,
we all scream
for ice cream!

COMFORT ZONE

How are you feeling right now? Hopefully more confident than before you reached for this book. One of the best ways to grow your confidence is to try new things—things that are out of your comfort zone. Your comfort zone includes things you do every day that aren't a challenge because you've done them so often that you're familiar and comfortable with doing them—you can almost do them without thinking!

Fill in the diagram on the opposite page with things in your comfort zone in the bubble at the top, and things most definitely out of your comfort zone—the no-go zone!—in the bubble at the bottom. Some examples have been added to get you started.

What things are you a little nervous about doing—things currently out of your comfort zone that you're really keen to try but don't feel quite ready to do? These are the things that go in the maybe zone in the middle—the bit that overlaps your comfort zone and your no-go zone!

Talk to your grown-up as they will have some great ideas for things to add—they know you very well!

Remember: stepping out of your comfort zone from time to time and trying new things will boost your self-belief.

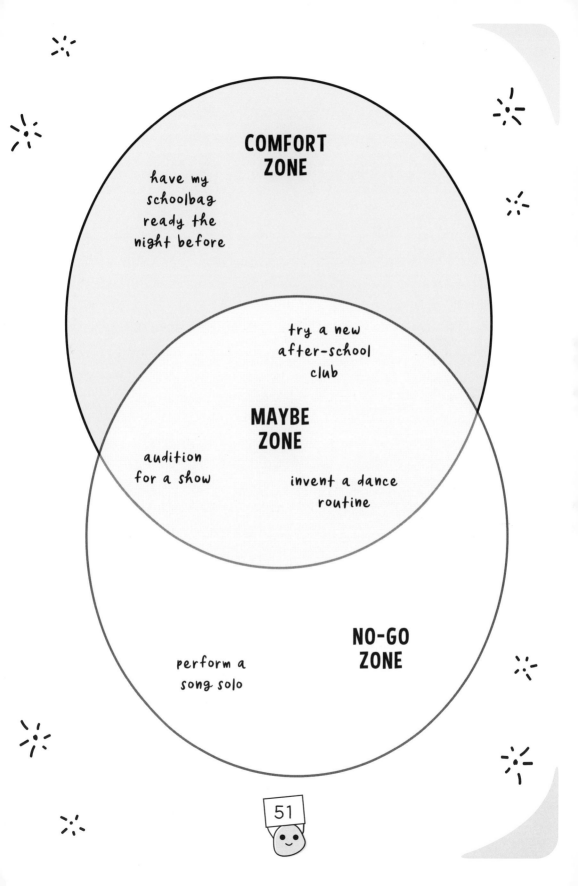

COMFORT ZONE

have my
schoolbag
ready the
night before

try a new
after-school
club

MAYBE ZONE

audition
for a show

invent a dance
routine

NO-GO ZONE

perform a
song solo

51

Climbing the confidence ladder

We face new challenges every day, and some can seem so big that we want to run in the opposite direction to avoid them! The best thing to do to make a challenge less scary is to break it down into steps so you can build up the confidence to tackle it.

Look at the ladder on the opposite page to see how a big challenge can be broken down into simple steps. Now use the empty ladder and write the thing you find most challenging at the top. Next, think about what smaller steps you can take to reach your goal and write them on each step—ask your grown-up to help if you like.

Building up your confidence with each step will equip you with the positive mindset needed to tackle any challenge with confidence.

Remember: anything worth doing will appear difficult at some stage. You may experience unexpected obstacles or challenges, but this means that when you accomplish your goal, the sense of achievement will be all the more wonderful.

Speak in front
of the class

Final
rehearsal the
night before

Practice in
front of your
family

Sing songs loudly
on the way to
school in the car

Practice in
front of your
grown-up

Read aloud
on your own

Setting small challenges and achieving them will boost your
confidence and grow your self-belief so that you can achieve
more and more new things. The sky really is the limit!

RELAX WITH MINDFULNESS

It's time to chill out after all that work you have put in so far. Relaxing is very important for our well-being. Being rested makes us feel calm in our minds and bodies and helps us stay happy and healthy.

Some people like to practice mindfulness to feel calm. Mindfulness means giving your full attention to the present moment and taking your time to slow down and feel calm. To look at it another way, mindfulness is the opposite of rushing about and doing lots of things at once!

Try this mindfulness exercise with your grown-up— you can write or draw your answers here.

Body sensations
What can you SEE?

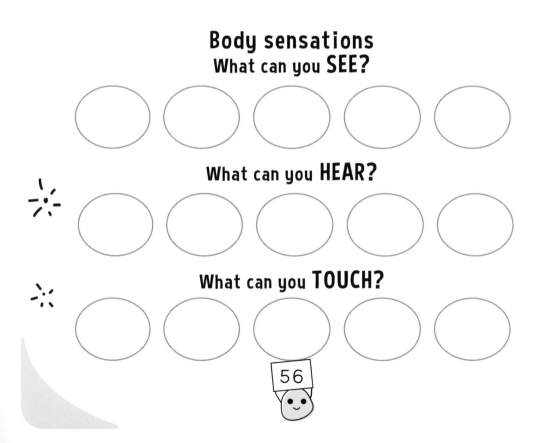

What can you HEAR?

What can you TOUCH?

What can you SMELL?

◯ ◯ ◯ ◯ ◯

How does your body FEEL?

◯ ◯ ◯ ◯ ◯

**Can you name these feelings in your body?
Circle the sensations and feelings below.**

warm   cold   happy   excited

shy   tired   grumpy   hungry

tense   calm   safe

Having a relaxed mind is very important for all aspects of your health. It can even help with learning because your attention span is boosted and you can think more creatively and constructively. This is why having a relaxed mind is great for solving math problems and making great art!

TAKE IN YOUR SURROUNDINGS

Here's another fun way to relax and be mindful. Get yourself a pencil and sketch the following things that you see around you by noticing small details that you might frequently overlook. Take your time and don't worry about making mistakes or being too precise about the result as the most important part of this exercise is to enjoy looking and observing.

Draw the following in the spaces provided:

Something hairy	Something lumpy	A cozy spot

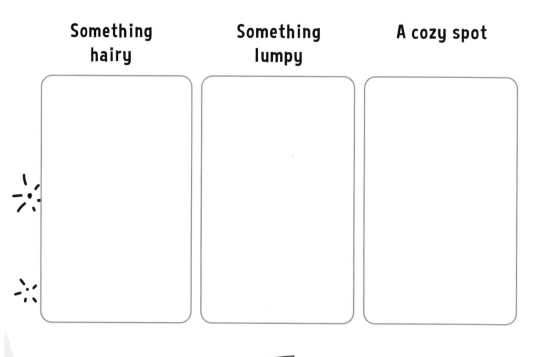

Something shiny

A close-up of a textured surface

The view above

The view below

The first thing you notice to your left

Something green

Yoga

Yoga is very calming, as it gently stretches your body and is one of the best ways to be mindful. It's also great for helping you sit up straight and pay attention in class, as well as standing tall so you feel more confident. It also makes you feel better by reducing worry and balancing your mood.

Practicing yoga encourages positive self-esteem and body awareness through a physical activity that's non-competitive.

Yoga has many health benefits and enhances flexibility, strength, and coordination. It also improves concentration and promotes a sense of calmness and relaxation.

Here are some simple yoga poses to try. Try to stay in each pose for 10 seconds—it's harder than you think! Have a yoga mat or comfy rug or blanket to lie on, and wear comfortable clothes, like shorts and a top.

MOUNTAIN POSE

Stand with your feet parallel and slightly apart
so that you can balance your weight evenly
between your feet. Reach your arms up into the
air, with your palms facing forward and your
fingers spread. Stand tall and strong.

61

HAPPY BABY POSE

Lie on your back and fold your knees so that they are touching your chest. Keep your knees where they are and stretch your feet up to the ceiling. Reach up between your knees with your hands and hold your feet. Now rock gently like a happy baby.

CAT POSE

Begin on your hands and knees, and make your back as flat as possible, like a tabletop. Make sure your hips are directly above your knees and your arms are straight, like table legs. Breathe out and round your back like a cat, and tuck in your head a little. Now breathe in and return to a flat back.

EASY POSE

This is a pose that you are probably quite familiar with. Sit on the floor and cross your legs, making sure the outer edges of your feet are resting on the floor with one foot on top of the other. Breathe out as you straighten your spine—this is easier to do if you can imagine an invisible thread being pulled up through the top of your head. Take a few breaths in this pose and feel your spine lengthening each time you breathe out. You can rest your hands in your lap or on your knees, with your palms facing up.

BRIDGE POSE

Lie on your back with your arms by your sides. Bend your knees, place your feet on the floor, and breathe out. Using the strength in your legs, lift your bottom off the floor, so you are making a sort of bridge, and tuck in your chin. Try to hold the pose for a few seconds before gently lowering your bottom back onto the floor when you next breathe out.

Make your bedroom into your ultimate chill-out zone

Having a comfy and cozy place to retreat to is important for when you need to relax and recharge. Draw out a plan of your bedroom—just the four walls, your window and door, and your bedroom furniture. Below are some things that can help you feel calm and relaxed. Draw these and anything else that appeals to you, and select a calming color palette before coloring in your ultimate chill-out zone.

COLORS

	Walls		Floor		Bed
	Cushions		Night light		Door

Lucky charms

Do you have a lucky charm? It could be any object—a small toy that can fit in your pocket, a favorite pair of socks or a hair tie—that you believe gives you a bit of a boost when you need it. Researchers have found that having a lucky charm can make you feel more confident!

If you don't have a lucky charm, try making this little medal. You can tie it to your bag or keep it in your pencil case— just make sure it's somewhere you will see it regularly so it's a constant reminder that you've got this!

You will need:
- Small square of card stock – approx. 1 in x 1 in
- Scissors
- Pens or pencils
- Glue
- Eco-friendly glitter
- String

1. Practice coloring in the designs on the facing page and think of a favorite word that could be written in the middle of your charm–it could be your name or perhaps a mantra from page 88.

2. Copy the outline of your favorite charm design onto the square of card and carefully cut it out and prick a hole for the string to be threaded through at the end.

3. Write your magic word in the middle of your charm and decorate around the word with pens, pencils, or paint.

4. Once dry, turn over your charm and place it on some newspaper. Cover the blank side of the charm with glue and shake the glitter.

5. Leave to dry before shaking off the excess glitter.

6. Thread the string through the hole and then thread the string through a zipper on a bag.

Pebbles also make great lucky charms, as you can tuck them in your hand for luck or when you want to feel brave. They're good fun to decorate too. Get your creativity flowing and see what charms you can make!

Feeling low in confidence can stop you from wanting to try new things. Something we haven't done before might make us worry that we'll make mistakes because it seems DIFFICULT or SCARY or maybe even a bit STRANGE. And when the worry alarm goes, off it can make you want to shrink away and not try those new things.

But did you know that every time you try something different or something new, your brain GROWS new connections? These connections are called neural pathways. The more you do the new things, the stronger these connections become—for example, you can recite the alphabet with no effort at all, and you can do your three times table because you've done it so many times. These pathways become the norm.

You can apply the same principle to any activity. So, the next time you're worried about trying something new, don't think about the possibility of making a mistake; instead, think of the new neural pathways being created in your brain!

The best way to encourage each other (you and your grown-up!) to have a growth mindset is to allow yourselves to be overheard when you are "thinking aloud" as you come up with positive ways to approach things that might be new to you. You can do it!

TRYING NEW THINGS = A BIGGER, MORE CONFIDENT BRAIN!

Trying new things will grow your brain by creating new neural pathways, which build your resilience and problem-solving skills so you feel more confident when faced with new challenges.

Imagine this brain represents your brain, and the more ideas and color it contains, the more confident you will feel. See how colorful and exciting you can make it! Write down big and small hopes and dreams on the dashed lines to create new neural pathways and color them in too! Visualizing these hopes and dreams means you're more likely to make them happen!

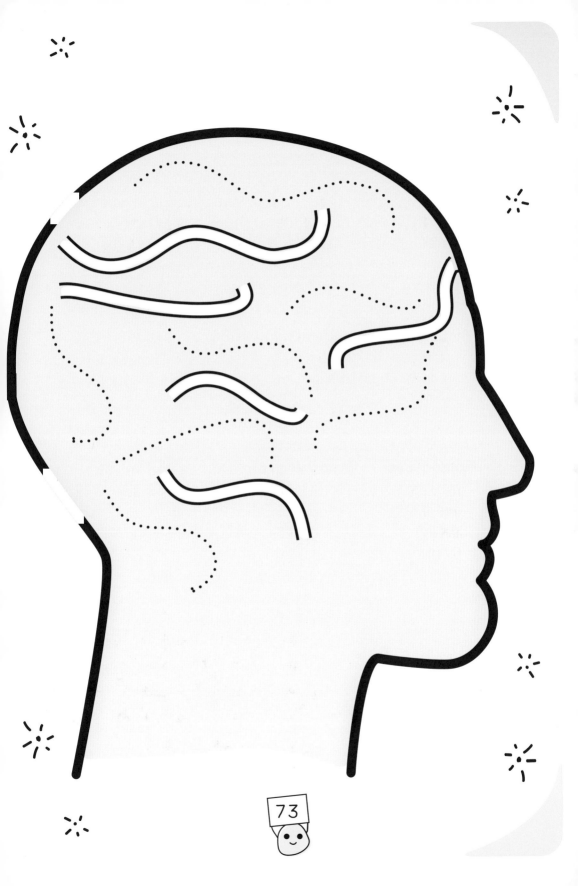

Keep an emotions diary

Sometimes it can help to record how you're feeling in different situations in order to find out if there is anything in particular that makes you feel negative emotions like worry, anger, or sadness, which can affect your self-confidence. There is nothing wrong with feeling these emotions—all emotions are okay and it means that you are healthy and emotionally strong.

Use this diary page to write down keywords or use emoji faces to show how you feel at various times each day for a week. If you find there is no emoji for how you feel, you can invent your own!

Here's an example diary:

Mon	Tues	Wed	Thurs	Fri	Sat	Sun
☹	😅	😅	😮	🙂	😊	😕

KEY

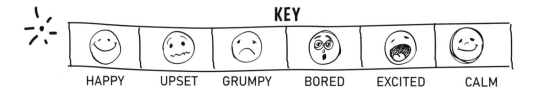

HAPPY   UPSET   GRUMPY   BORED   EXCITED   CALM

Mon	Tues	Wed	Thurs	Fri	Sat	Sun

Drawing your emotions helps you become aware of how you're feeling in the present moment. Try this activity at different times of the day. If you're struggling for ideas, talk with your grown-up and think about words that come to mind. They don't have to be specific feelings like "happy" or "sad"; maybe you feel "itchy" or "sunny" or something like that. These words are a window on how you're feeling inside.

Role models

Who are your role models? It could be someone you know like a parent, a caregiver, a teacher, or maybe a sibling, or perhaps it's a public figure like an athlete, an environmental activist, or a singer.

Write down the person or people that you look up to and why. What is it about them that makes them stand out to you?

Draw their faces in the spaces and write about their strengths and achievements, and what makes them exceptional.

Having role models who have achieved incredible things can help inspire you to believe in yourself and your abilities. Because if they can do it, so can you! Here are a couple of great examples of young people who have achieved great things despite setbacks.

Marcus Rashford MBE (born 1997) began his soccer career at the age of five! He came from a low-income family but that didn't stop him from reaching for his dream of becoming an international soccer player. He used his fame for good, ensuring free school meals for all children in schools during the pandemic. He has also set up community support programs, promotes children's reading and literacy, and campaigns for diversity and inclusion and against racism and homelessness.

At just 15 years of age, **Greta Thunberg** (born 2003) became the voice of a new generation of environmental activists after her one-person protest outside the Swedish Parliament for action on climate change. She has experienced poor mental health from a young age but has fought her personal difficulties and negative people and is now recognized as a key figure in the global fight against climate change. She has received three nominations for the Nobel Peace Prize in three years. She is the youngest person ever to be named *TIME*'s Person of the Year, in 2019.

WRITE A LETTER TO YOUR ROLE MODEL

What would you say to your role model if you could, and what would you ask them? Sometimes learning more about how a person has overcome difficulties and achieved what they have—be it sporting success, going into space, being successful in business, or gaining recognition for championing an important social or environmental cause—can help motivate us to achieve our own hopes and dreams.

Think about who you would write to and what you might ask them and write it on the letter on the facing page. You can cut it out when you have finished and send it to them.

Dear

BE YOUR OWN ROLE MODEL!

Let's face it, you are pretty awesome! What do you think you will be like in ten years' time? Why not write a letter to your future self? What would you ask? What things are important to you now that you don't want **future you** to ever forget?

Here are some ideas to get you thinking:

Describe what your bedroom is like now, and your hopes for what it will be like in ten years' time.

Who is your best friend or your favorite person now? What do you think they will be like ten years from now? Will you still be doing the same things, do you think?

Where will you be in ten years?

What are your goals for the future?

What are your favorite things and hobbies now?
Do you expect them to be the same in the future?

What will FUTURE YOU look like? Draw a picture.

When you have written your letter, store it somewhere safe so it's ready for **future you** to read ten years from now. What will the date be when you can finally read the letter? Add the date here:

Looking to the future and visualizing it can make you feel more confident about the unknowns that lie ahead. It can also make for fascinating reading in ten years' time! Why not imagine a future you that you really admire and write a reply from future you back to you, describing what really matters to future you!

Get out in nature

Being outside is great fun—there's so much more space to run around and let off steam. But there's more to it than that because being outside and connecting with nature every day is good for your physical and mental well-being too. It makes you feel calmer and quiets your mind, soothing away worries. It also provides a confidence boost—being around nature helps you feel part of something bigger and can help you feel ready to take on new challenges.

Where do you like to go and what do you like to do when you're out in nature?

Write the places and fun things to do in the great outdoors among the trees.

82

The therapeutic benefits of spending time among trees is taken very seriously in Japan. They call it "forest bathing," and it is prescribed by doctors for all manner of ailments. Spending time in nature is scientifically proven to boost your immune system.

GO ON A RAINBOW WALK

This is a simple mindfulness exercise that can be enjoyed at any time of year and helps you feel present and notice your surroundings. It's also a fun game to play with your grown-up. The idea is simple: go for a walk and look for something red, then orange, then yellow, then green, blue, indigo, and violet. Then start again and repeat the rainbow until you have finished your walk.

You can draw your finds on this page too!

Another fun color-themed game to play with your grown-up is to follow one color, for example yellow. You could see a yellow bike and follow it until you see a yellow flower, then a yellow sign, a yellow gate, etc. and see where you end up. You might see a whole new part of where you live and discover details that you didn't know existed! You could also do a mini version of this activity around your home.

Try some green exercise

"Green" exercise is any physical activity that you do outdoors, in nature, such as in your backyard, local park or woods, or by the sea. Being in natural surroundings makes you feel calm and balanced and content.

What sort of green exercise could you try? Here are some ideas and some space to add your own activities.

Swimming or paddling in the sea

Skipping in the grass

Cartwheels and circus skills in the park

Balancing

Trampolining

Playing soccer

Make your own mantras

A mantra may sound like a type of snake, but is in fact something entirely different! A mantra is a powerful word, phrase, or sound that can change the way you feel inside. Mantras can make you feel calm, strong, and confident and can help prepare you to feel and do your best. A mantra can be something short and simple like, "Stay strong," "Be calm," or "I can do this." Repeating a mantra, either in your head or out loud, can shape how you feel so you feel confident in yourself and your abilities.

There is no one better to be than me.

I am enough.

I am an amazing person.

I get better every single day.

Today I am a leader.

All of my problems have solutions.

I forgive myself for my mistakes.

88

Here are some positive mantras to try with your grown-up.

Write your own mantras here and say them
to yourself whenever you need them.

Saying out loud, thinking, or writing
down your mantras is a great confidence
booster. Repeat them regularly so that
it becomes a positive, mood-boosting habit,
like the neural pathways on page 70.

89

DREAM BIG— VISION BOARD

The sky really is the limit and a technique that some experts use to help them dream big is something called visualization. To visualize your future is to create a picture in your mind of you achieving your biggest dreams, making this picture as vivid as you can imagine. Doing this can help you focus on the things that you want to achieve and do. An even more fun way of visualizing your dreams is to create a vision board, with beautiful pictures and meaningful words that you can look at to make you feel strong and happy about yourself and your hopes and dreams.

Use these pages for your vision board. Start by cutting out images from magazines or drawing images of the types of things that you want to achieve. For example, if you have hopes of being an Olympian, cut out a stadium or an athlete, or if you want to cycle around the world, draw a bike wheel and a world and add the names of the countries you wish to visit. Maybe you'd like to work with animals or have a pet one day—if so, add images of your ideal pet.

Thinking about your future in this way will give you the confidence boost you need to reach for your dreams!

91

Funny stuff

Laughing is very good for you. It releases endorphins, which make you feel happy, but it's good for your health too! A good giggle is like exercising, because it gets your blood flowing and your muscles working. Scientists have even discovered that it reduces worry, improves your memory, and can help you sleep better and make you feel strong and happy.

Did you know that the average child laughs 400 times a day? Why don't you challenge yourself to laugh even more times than this! Try answering some of these questions. You can write down your answers or talk about them with your grown-up and watch them split their sides with laughter too!

What's the funniest joke you've ever heard about chickens? Can you come up with an even funnier one?

Who makes you laugh the most and why? What score would you give them on the laugh-o-meter?

What's the funniest thing that's happened at school this year?

What makes you laugh until you fall over?

Who is the silliest person in your family? Can you think of anything sillier?!

HEALTHY SNACK FACES

Everyone loves sugar but it can also make you feel grumpy and unhappy, which can lead to low confidence.

So next time you are feeling hungry for a snack, reach for some healthier options that will boost your energy and make you feel great too.

Try these ideas for size. The only rule is that the components need to be healthy and they must make a face!

Here are some ideas for facial features, or be creative and find your own:

Facial outline — thin slices of bell pepper, sunflower seeds, goji berries, raisins, avocado

Eyes — kiwi slices, banana slices, orange segments with an olive in the middle

Nose — half a strawberry, pointy end of a carrot, two raspberries, half a grape, dollop of hummus!

Mouth — slice of watermelon or apple, a whole banana (make sure it's extra bendy!), a mandarin segment for a very small smile!

Teeth — coconut cubes, chopped mango, pineapple, or carrot

Hair — dried seaweed, trail mix, sliced strawberry, carrot sticks

See if you can make a self-portrait out of fruit, veg, nuts, and seeds!

Silly time!

Congratulations, you have won 5 silly minutes to let yourself go!
What will you do?

Here are some very silly ideas:

make your way across the room like a caterpillar

drink from a bowl

sing a funny song

sing your favorite song in a low voice

make farm animal noises

do a silly dance

ADD YOUR OWN VERY
SILLY IDEAS HERE!

When our feelings build or become uncomfortable, it's important to release that pressure in some way, and one of the best ways is to let off steam! Letting off steam can mean different things to different people — it could be a crazy 5 minutes of jumping up and down to your favorite song, playing with a pet, or throwing a ball against a wall. You'll find that you're more likely to feel relaxed and more positive afterward, so you can feel on top of the world! What sort of things can you think of to let off steam? See if you can add to the ideas on the page.

THE SMILE-A-DAY JOURNAL

Being grateful for all the good things in your life that make you smile is a great way to feel confident about yourself every day. What sort of things come to mind when you think about what makes you smile? It could be time that you spend with your family or friends, or activities you enjoy doing, or cuddling a pet, or a funny joke that you hear—there's no rule as to how big or small these things can be, as long as they make you smile!

Start your smile-a-day journal by noting three things that made you smile today. Make it part of your bedtime routine so you go to bed with happy thoughts each night, and you will soon feel more confident and positive every single day, just by remembering the happy moments of your day. Recalling a happy memory brings that happy emotion forward so you experience the joy of it all over again.

Day	Smile 1	Smile 2	Smile 3
Monday			
Tuesday			
Wednesday			
Thursday			
Friday			
Saturday			
Sunday			

Day	Smile 1	Smile 2	Smile 3
Monday			
Tuesday			
Wednesday			
Thursday			
Friday			
Saturday			
Sunday			

Day	Smile 1	Smile 2	Smile 3
Monday			
Tuesday			
Wednesday			
Thursday			
Friday			
Saturday			
Sunday			

Just breathe

When we're feeling low in confidence, we can experience all sorts of uncomfortable physical sensations, like fast breathing, sweating, muddled thoughts, and butterflies in the tummy. We can even feel tearful. That's a lot of not-very-nice feelings.

The quickest and simplest way to soothe these uncomfortable feelings and restore calmness to your mind and body is to take some calming breaths. Here's how to do it. Try it with your grown-up and see how much calmer you feel:

- Sit down comfortably. Place one hand on your tummy just below your ribcage, then place your other hand in the middle of your chest.
- Breathe in deeply through your nostrils for 3 seconds and allow your first hand to be pushed out by your stomach.

- Hold this for 2 seconds.
- Breathe out through your mouth for 4 seconds.
- Repeat up to 10 times.

HERE'S A BREATHING EXERCISE YOU CAN DO WITH A SLICE OF PIZZA!

Everyone loves pizza, right? What are your favorite toppings? Draw them on this pizza slice here—maybe some cheese, tomatoes, sweet peppers, ham—put it all on there and color it in.

That looks mouth-watering! Now imagine the smell of that fresh slice of pizza and take a deep breath in through your nose to inhale all those smells. Then, slowly breathe out through your mouth to cool your pizza slice ready for eating.

STOP!

Sometimes, in order to feel calm, confident, and in control, we need to stop what we're doing and take a moment to ourselves. This is a really good way to slow down the busyness going on around us and to notice how we're feeling.

STOP stands for:

Stop what you're doing and find a quiet place to calm yourself.

Take a few calming breaths.

Observe your thoughts and notice feelings in your body.

Proceed by either carrying on with what you were doing, or by changing what you were doing if it helps you.

Try this out with your grown-up so you feel comfortable doing it when you need to. There is no time limit on how long or short a time you take—it's about what feels right for you.

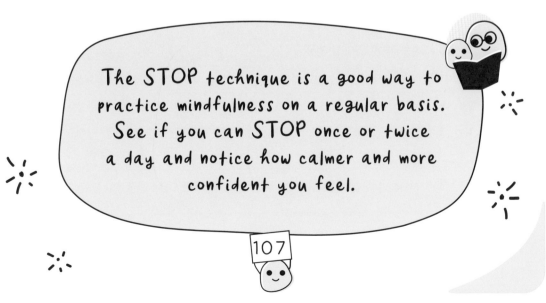

The STOP technique is a good way to practice mindfulness on a regular basis. See if you can STOP once or twice a day and notice how calmer and more confident you feel.

Take time to unwind

When you're feeling worried or nervous, it can seem like you're tied up in knots or scrunched up tight due to the tension you're feeling in your body. Here's a way to unwind by moving your body as if you are unwinding! You can do this standing up or sitting down.

Start with your arms — imagine they are two big whisks mixing a cake and rotate them slowly. Start with small rotations and gradually make them bigger, because it's going to be a very big cake!

Wrists — now roll your wrists slowly, as if you're adding the cake mix and smoothing it into the tin.

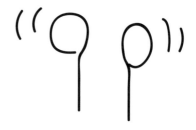

Legs — this is a bit trickier and requires good balance. While waiting for your cake to bake in the oven, circle one leg five times in one direction and then the other — yes, you need to raise it off the ground! Then switch to the other leg.

Feet — rotate your feet at the ankle, first one way then the other. Switch feet and repeat.

Shoulders — it's time to get ready to lift out the cake from the oven — you're going to need to get your shoulders ready! Rotate your shoulders back five times and then forward.

Hips — the cake is finally ready and it's time to do a victory body roll by unwinding your body at the hips — first in one direction and then the other. You've got it!

Sleep yourself confident

Sleep is essential to feeling healthy, happy, and confident. When we are asleep we rest, grow, heal, and get stronger physically and mentally. When we're feeling nervous or worried, though, it can make it hard to fall asleep, but there are some helpful things you can do to prepare you for restful sleep. The first is to have a regular routine before you go to sleep. Your routine might look something like this:

- Get your stuff ready for the next day.
- Have a bath.
- Get into your pajamas.
- Have a warm drink.
- Read a story—either your grown-up reads to you or you read to yourself.
- Draw or write in a journal or diary (see page 74).
- Say your goodnights and turn out the lights.
- Close your eyes.

Write your routine here:

If after a few days you are still finding it difficult
to sleep, try these things:

**Talk to your
grown-up about
anything that's
worrying you.**

**Avoid electronic gadgets
before bed–the bright
light on a gadget can trick
your brain into thinking
it's still daytime and
keep you wide awake.**

**Tidy your room–
a messy room can
make it harder
to sleep.**

**Try to go to bed at the
same time each night—
so your body soon learns
that it's time to switch
off at the same time
every night.**

**No midnight feasts!
Sugar will wake your
brain up and think
there's a party to
go to!**

Try some of these sleepy puzzles

Help Kip find his pillow

Complete the wordsearch

Dream
Doze
Nap
Rest
Snooze

t	p	c	a	d	r	n	i
e	d	r	e	a	m	p	q
c	o	n	x	m	u	a	k
e	z	o	o	n	s	p	y
f	e	t	p	j	l	w	n
a	w	q	s	m	o	r	p
r	l	n	c	e	t	x	a
o	v	e	p	w	r	m	n

112

Find the matching pair

Spot the 5 differences

Answers

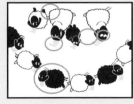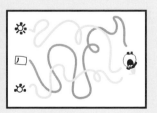

SPEND TIME WITH A FURRY FRIEND

Spending time with a pet is great fun—for you (and the pet!). Whether you have a guinea pig, a rabbit, a cat, or a dog, or maybe something more unusual, like a snake or gecko, petting an animal can make you feel happy and calm. This is because when you have the responsibility of looking after another living thing and its well-being and happiness, you feel their happiness too. Knowing that you have the skills to keep another living thing safe and well is a wonderful confidence booster! In addition, cuddling a pet helps you feel comforted, and pets can be very good listeners!

If you don't have a pet of your own, though, you can always spend time with other people's pets (with the owner's permission, of course) or perhaps your school has a pet that you can help care for.

What would be your perfect pet? Answer these questions to find out and then draw it on the facing page.

What do they eat?

What sort of noise do they make?

Do they need to go for walks?

Do they have fur, feathers, or fins?

Can they fit in your pocket?

What will you name them?

Are they cuddly?

Are they bigger than you?

What color are they?

DRAW YOUR DREAM PET HERE

Having a pet has been proven
to have many benefits to a young
person's self-esteem and self-confidence.
This is due to the interaction and
reciprocal nature of having an emotional
connection with an animal and being
part of its everyday care, well-being,
and development.

Be your own cheerleader

What do you like most about yourself? Don't be shy! You'll find some clues in what other people admire about you. See if you can answer these questions:

What do your friends ask you to help them with?

What are you really good at?

What are you most proud of?

What can you do that no one else can?

What's your favorite feature of your face?

What is your best subject at school?

Turning the spotlight on yourself can be a surprisingly challenging thing to do, but it's important to appreciate yourself. Keep this list where you can refer to it easily when you need a confidence boost, and add to it when you think of something new. Be your own cheerleader as you value all that you contribute to the world.

Awards cabinet

Whenever you do something brave, you need to mark it in some way so the memory stays with you. An award is a great thing to have, as it serves as a physical reminder that you can look at whenever you want to feel pride in your achievements.

Here's a cabinet full of shiny awards and they're all for you! But what are these awards for? Only you can decide. It could be for being a brilliant friend, singing a song at a family event, or winning a drawing contest. These awards are for things that you are super-proud of and want to remember forever!

MY CONFIDENCE TOOLKIT

Take a look back at all the activities in this book and make a note of the things that have been most helpful to you in feeling more confident.

Once you have finished the list, you can cut it out and keep it in a safe place to refer to whenever you need it. Maybe make a copy so you can have one on your wall in your bedroom and one in your backpack.

120

I Can Do

Amazing Things!

Conclusion

Confidence is something that takes time and dedication to grow, and using the skills learned in this book should go a long way to helping you feel more confident. Having the courage to believe in yourself and your abilities is something that will help you throughout your life. Confidence will grow the more you use it, like a muscle, so keep looking back at the activities as a reminder to practice positive self-talk, make eye-contact, get talking, set yourself small challenges, and, most importantly, dream big!

And always remember: you can do it!

The Worry Workbook:
A Kid's Activity Book for Dealing with Anxiety

Imogen Harrison

Paperback

ISBN: 978-1-5107-6407-1

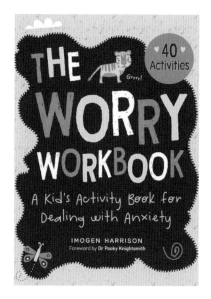

Worries come in all shapes and sizes, creeping up on us when we least expect them. Worries, and anxiety in general, are like little clouds floating above our heads that seem menacing and threatening at first glance. These clouds stop us from going places and doing things we really want and ruining the fun days we have planned.

With *The Worry Workbook*, children ages 8 to 12 will learn about how worrying affects their bodies, are encouraged to listen to their thoughts, and are invited to try activities that will help them push through their worries and anxieties, coming out the other side ready to tackle the world. Activities include:

- Making a worry camera that captures fears and shrinks them into a manageable size
- Coloring in a mood tracker that explores the rainbow of everyday emotions
- Writing on the magic mirror of compliments to help recognize their strengths
- Creating their very own list of anti-worry actions to fight fear and keep smiling

Parents: This book has been peer reviewed by a child psychologist, who has left notes throughout just in case your child has questions about the activities provided.

Look for these other helpful titles from Sky Pony Press!

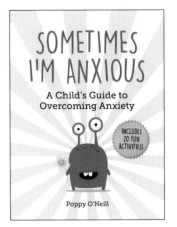

Paperback
ISBN: 978-1-5107-4748-7

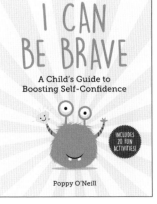

Paperback
ISBN: 978-1-5107-6408-8

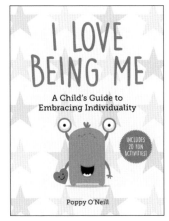

Paperback
ISBN: 978-1-5107-6409-5

Paperback
ISBN: 978-1-5107-4747-0

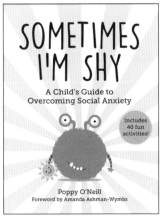

Paperback
ISBN: 978-1-5107-7062-1

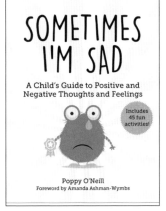

Paperback
ISBN: 978-1-5107-7273-1

Image credits: